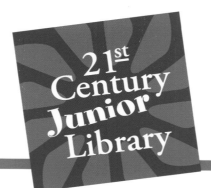

21ˢᵗ Century Junior Library

What is a Plant

by Jennifer Colby

CHERRY LAKE PUBLISHING * ANN ARBOR, MICHIGAN

Published in the United States of America by Cherry Lake Publishing
Ann Arbor, Michigan
www.cherrylakepublishing.com

Consultants: Elizabeth A. Glynn, Youth Education Coordinator, Matthaei Botanical
Gardens and Nichols Arboretum, University of Michigan; Marla Conn, ReadAbility, Inc.

Photo Credits: © pan demin/Shutterstock Images, cover; © Neirfy/Shutterstock Images, 4; © TFoxFoto/
Shutterstock Images, 6; © cosmin4000/Thinkstock, 8; © Christopher Boswell/Shutterstock Images, 10;
© Chokniti Khongchum/Shutterstock Images, 12; © Lubava/Shutterstock Images, 14; © Filipe B.
Varela/ Shutterstock Images, 16; © Dudakova Elena /Shutterstock Images, 18; © Darryl Sleath /
Shutterstock Images, 20

LIBRARY OF CONGRESS CATALOGING-IN-PUBLICATION DATA
Colby, Jennifer, 1971-
  What is a plant?/by Jennifer Colby. – [Revised edition]
    pages cm.—(21st century junior library)
  Includes bibliographical references and index.
  ISBN 978-1-63188-042-1 (hardcover)—ISBN 978-1-63188-128-2 (pdf)—
ISBN 978-1-63188-085-8 (pbk.)—ISBN 978-1-63188-171-8 (ebook)
  1. Plants–Juvenile literature. I. Title. II. Series: 21st century junior library.
  QK49.C64 2014
  580–dc23   2014006229

Cherry Lake Publishing would like to acknowledge the work of
The Partnership for 21st Century Skills.
Please visit www.p21.org for more information.

Printed in the United States of America

CONTENTS

There are many different kinds of plants.

Plants Everywhere

Can you name one kind of plant? Did you say a sunflower? Or maybe your answer is an oak tree. You might even think of a cactus! Guess what? You are right!

A cactus grows where it is hot and dry.

A sunflower, an oak tree, and a cactus do not look the same. But they are all plants. Let's look closer and see what plants have in common.

leaves

stem

roots

Most plants have roots, stems, and leaves.

Roots, Stems, and Leaves

All plants have three things in common. Plants are living things, but they don't move around. They make their own food. They grow and make new plants.

Almost all plants have three basic parts: **roots**, **stems**, and **leaves**.

Tree trunks are big, stiff stems.

Most roots grow down into the dirt. They absorb water from the dirt. Roots also help keep the plant steady in the ground.

Stems carry water from the roots up to the leaves. Stems also carry food made by the leaves back to the rest of the plant. Some stems are hard and stiff. Other stems are green and can bend.

Leaves come in different colors, shapes, and sizes.

A plant needs many leaves to make its food. Leaves use water, air, and the energy from sunlight to make food for the plant.

Think!

Plants are just one kind of living thing. Animals are another kind of living thing. Can you think of two ways plants and animals are the same? Can you think of two ways they are different?

A seed has a tiny plant inside of it.

Growing New Plants

Have you ever seen a seed? You have probably eaten a **seed**. An almond is a seed you can eat. Can you think of other kinds of seeds?

Inside each seed is a tiny plant. The tiny plant is called an **embryo**. The seed will grow into a new plant if it has the things it needs.

The roots of a plant absorb water.

A seed needs water, air, and sunlight to grow into a new plant. A plant grows roots to reach down into the dirt to get water. A plant grows stems to reach up toward the sun.

Make a Guess!

How many seeds do you think you will find in a piece of fruit? Make a guess. Then ask an adult to help you cut up a piece of fruit. An apple, orange, or pear will work best. Find all of the seeds inside. Count them. How close was your guess to the number of seeds you found?

The stems of plants grow toward the sun.

A plant grows leaves on its stems to get air and sunlight.

Now the plant has water, air, and sunlight. Plants need all three things to grow.

Create!

Drawing pictures can be a good way to remember what you have learned. Pick one kind of plant. Draw a picture of it. Be sure to label its roots, stems, and leaves.

Growing your own plants will help you learn more about them.

Grow and Learn

Do you want to learn more about plants? Plant some seeds! In the summer, you can have a garden outside. In the winter, you can grow seeds in a pot indoors.

Make sure your plants have what they need to grow. Do you remember what plants need to grow? Did you say water, air, and sunlight? Then you are on your way to being a plant **expert**!

GLOSSARY

embryo (EM-bree-oh) a tiny plant inside a seed that will develop if the conditions are right

expert (EK-spurt) a person who knows everything about a subject

identify (eye-DEN-tuh-fye) to tell what something is or who someone is

leaves (LEEVZ) the parts of plants that soak up sunlight and make food for the plant

librarian (lye-BRAR-ee-uhn) a person who works in a library and helps people find books and information

roots (ROOTS) the parts of plants that soak up water and minerals, usually underground

seed (SEED) the part of a plant that can grow into a new plant

stems (STEMZ) the parts of plants that carry water and minerals to the leaves and carry food to the rest of the plant

FIND OUT MORE

BOOKS

Burnie, David. *Eyewitness Plant.* New York: DK Publishing, 2011.

Lawrence, Ellen. *Freaky Plant Facts: Extreme Greens.* New York: Bearport Publishing, 2013.

WEB SITES

Missouri Botanical Garden—Biology of Plants
www.mbgnet.net/bioplants/main.html
Learn how plants are living things just like humans and animals.

University of Illinois Extension—The Great Plant Escape
http://urbanext.illinois.edu/gpe/index.cfm
Learn some amazing mysteries of plant life.

INDEX

ABOUT THE AUTHOR

Jennifer Colby is a school librarian, and she also has a bachelor's degree in Landscape Architecture. By writing these books, she has combined her talents for two of her favorite things. She likes to garden and grow her own food. In June she makes strawberry jam for her children to enjoy all year long.